Beat the Record

Written by

James Harrison

Edited by

Graham Marks

Designed by

Jonathan Lambert

Illustrated by

Gary Andrews

© **Guinness Superlatives Ltd. 1986**

Published in Great Britain by Guinness Superlatives Ltd.,
33 London Road, Enfield, Middlesex EN2 6DJ

**Produced for the Publishers by
Keith Faulkner Publishing Ltd.**

**'Guinness' is a registered trade mark of Guinness
Superlatives Ltd.**

British Library Cataloguing in Publication Data
Beat the record.
  1. Games——Juvenile literature
  2. Children's parties——Juvenile literature
    793.2'1   GV1203
ISBN 0–85112–829–7

Typeset by Kalligraphics Ltd. Printed in Great Britain by
R. J. Acford, Chichester, Sussex

Beat the Record

GUINNESS BOOKS

Lest we forget

In 1974 a Bhuddist monk, by the name of Bhandanta Vicitsara, recited 16,000 pages of religious text at one go – without peeking! He was a rare case of a man with eidetic (photographic) memory. As most of us frequently suffer from blank memory, it might be better to start on something smaller. **After reading this text, close the book and see how much you can recite – *without peeking.***

Number cruncher!

An Indian lady, Mrs. Shakuntala Devi, multiplied two random 13 digit numbers picked by the Computer Department of the Imperial College, London. She got the correct answer – 18,947,668,177,995,426,462,773,730 – in only 28 seconds! **Starting with small numbers and whilst timing yourself, multiply them together. Then challenge your friends to do better, increasing the numbers to be multiplied every go.**

1. ON YOUR MARKS, GET SET...

2. RECITE...

Not so fast!

In a world where everything seems to get faster all the time, even talking is the subject of record-breaking speeds. Few people, it has been found, are able to speak articulately at speeds of 300 words or more per minute. One record that has never been beaten is that of saying Hamlet's 262 word 'Soliloquy' in under 24 seconds – **so why not have a go and see how fast you can get? A tape recorder might be handy, as well as a stopwatch, if you start getting really fast.**

1. SHAKEY... SHAKEY...

2. FIZZ... BANG... FIZZ.

What a corker!

Where else but in America could they afford to experiment with champagne? Possibly in a champagne factory; but it was in Reno, Nevada that Peter Kirby won the 1981 world record for a champagne cork flight – 105ft 9in (32.23m). **We're not suggesting this as an everyday game but when you try for the record, do have some glasses at the ready.**

SAIPPUAKIVIKAUPPIAS

Back to front

A palindrome is a word that reads the same left to right as right to left. Although people make them up, they do appear naturally in national languages. The longest, 19 letters, is in the Finnish language; it means 'someone who sells caustic soda' and here it is: 'saippuakivikauppias'. **Try inventing one, but give yourself a time limit.**

Stand still laddie!

The longest that anyone has continuously remained motionless is 13 hr by Willie Nugent, 37, at *The Guinness World of Records* permanent exhibition at the Trocadero, Piccadilly, London, on 24 June 1985.

1. INSPECT THE TARGET...

3. KEEP AN EYE ON YOUR WORK...

How apeeling

The record for the longest single unbroken apple peel is held by Kathy Wafler, of New York State, USA. In 11hrs 30mins she peeled a 172ft 4in (52.51m) strip off a 20oz (567g) apple. **As most of us don't have 11 hours to spare the best way to have a go at this record is to choose apples of approximately the same size and give a time limit to the assembled peelers.**

2. START PEELING...

Up and away

On the 21 May 1972, Jane Dorst let go her toy balloon from Atherton, California, USA... 20 days later it floated down – guess where? No, not Atherton, but Africa! An incredible 14,500km (9,000mls) away! **If the winds are favourable, get yourself a helium balloon and go for it, but don't forget to attach a self-addressed label!**

Footless & fancy free

Mr. V. S. Kumar Anandan of Colombo, Sri Lanka has actually got two legs, complete with feet, but in May 1980 he did without one of the pair and stood for 33hrs on one foot. The rules of this particular sport – popular among birds – are that the other foot may not be rested on the standing one, and no object may be used for balance or support. *Have a go!*

Breakdancin' beer mats

Here's a neat feat to compete with if you have a deft hand and a sharp eye – place a beer mat half on/half off the edge of a table. Flip it over (the mat, not the table) with the back of your fingers and catch it with the same hand – before it hits the tabletop. **Sounds easy? Maybe with one, but try 10 and you'll still be 57 short of the record set by 18 year old Darren Ault in 1985!**

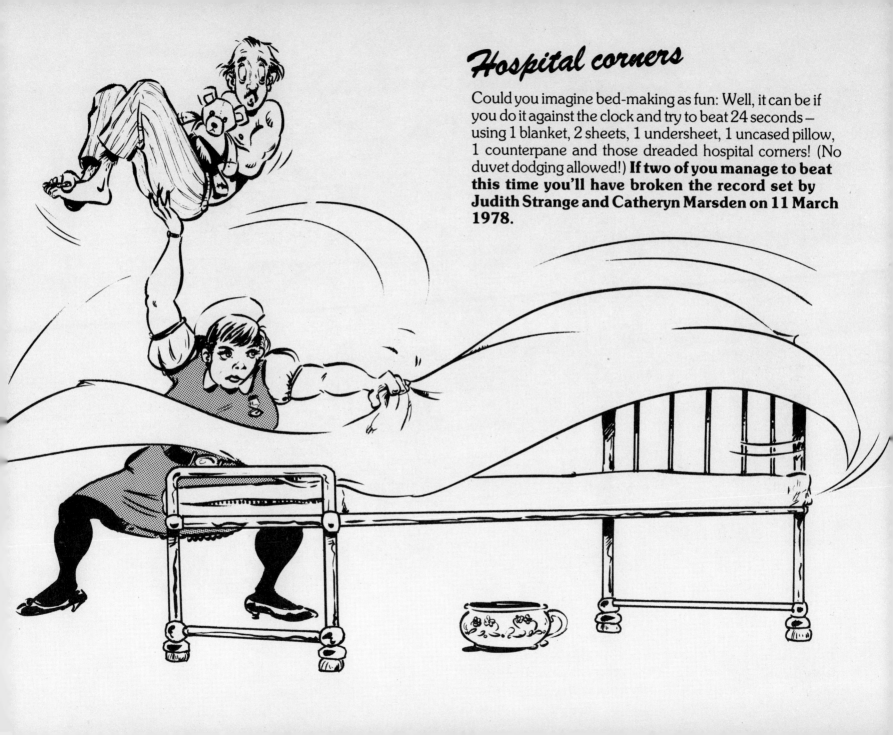

Hospital corners

Could you imagine bed-making as fun: Well, it can be if you do it against the clock and try to beat 24 seconds – using 1 blanket, 2 sheets, 1 undersheet, 1 uncased pillow, 1 counterpane and those dreaded hospital corners! (No duvet dodging allowed!) **If two of you manage to beat this time you'll have broken the record set by Judith Strange and Catheryn Marsden on 11 March 1978.**

Thick as a brick

David and Kym Barger, from Missouri, USA, each carried one 4.053kg (8lb 15oz) brick – held in a downward pinch – for a staggering 72.4km (45mls) on 21 May 1977. The feminine record is 30.89km (19.2mls) with a 4.42kg (9lb 12oz) brick carried by Cynthia Ann Smolko on 14 May 1977. **To have a go at this record, stake out an area of garden or park and see who can manage the most lengths. No swapping hands or cradling the brick!**

Square shot putter

Olympic shot-putter Geoff Capes threw a 2.2kg (5lb) brick 44.5m (146ft) at Braybrook School, Cambs., UK, in 1978 – thus creating the world brick-throwing record! **Be careful if you try to 'break' this record – choose an open space, nuzzle the brick under your chin and throw shot-put style.**

Brick a back

A back-breaking record with bricks was set by Alan Keates on 15 May 1984. He laid out 26 bricks horizontally – making a span of 168.9cm (66½in) – and then lifted them up in a line! The bricks weighed 58.76kg (130lb). **To try this out yourself, start with five bricks and work your way up slowly into the record books!**

Wheelie, or won't he?

If you thought you were hot at wheelies on your BMX, then just imagine a wheelie lasting 1 hours, 16 minutes and 54 seconds! Englishman Craig Strong biked into the record books in 1983 with this time – and he wasn't even on a unicycle! **You won't be able to manage an hour first off, but why not see who amongst your friends can achieve the best times – starting at 30 seconds.**

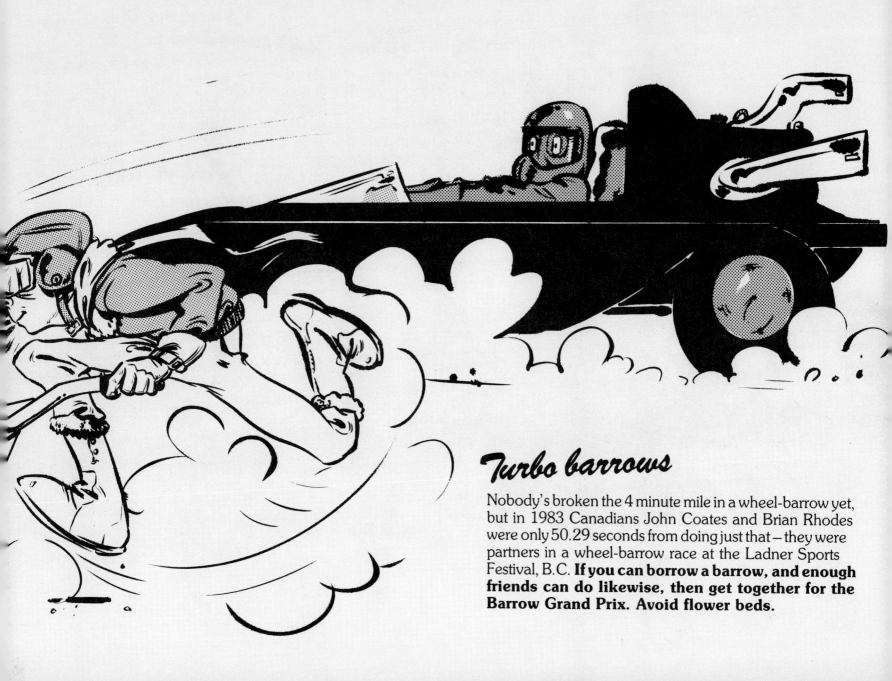

Turbo barrows

Nobody's broken the 4 minute mile in a wheel-barrow yet, but in 1983 Canadians John Coates and Brian Rhodes were only 50.29 seconds from doing just that — they were partners in a wheel-barrow race at the Ladner Sports Festival, B.C. **If you can borrow a barrow, and enough friends can do likewise, then get together for the Barrow Grand Prix. Avoid flower beds.**

2. CHEW, CHEW, CHEW...

3. BLOW, BLOW, BLOW...

1. CHOOSE YOUR GUM...

Long distance dealing

It must have been an interesting game of 'Snap' when Kevin St Onge threw a standard playing card 56.41m (185ft 1in), on 12 June 1979. It's obviously all in the wrist-snapping action! **Get a pack of cards, a large room, and start practising — you'll find you've got a long way to go to catch Kevin!**

Bubblegum balloon

Without getting sticky bubblegum all over her face, 18 year old Susan Montgomery managed to blow a 48.9cm (19.5in) diameter bubble in Fresno, California, USA. **To have a go, all you need is a standard amount of gum, some friends and a lot of puff — as well as access to plenty of soap and water!**

Balancing the budget

Canadian coin-balancer Bruce McConachy stacked a 205 25 cent piece column of coins on top of a Canadian Commemorative coin which was freestanding *vertically* on the base of another coin! Phew! Now that's a hard currency act to follow. **See how many coins you can hoard *up* without them toppling *over* – leave the vertical bit for later!**

Snatch 'n' grab

On 16 February 1985, at the *Guinness World of Records*, London, Andrew Gleed flipped 70 10p coins from the back of his forearm and caught them all clean in the same palm – so breaking his own world coin-snatching record! **If you think you can do better, try it – but don't break anything when you drop the coins!**

BAH! HUMBUG!

Grovel, grovel

Scraping one knee along the ground, then the other, Chris Lock of Bristol, UK, actually crawled – out of choice – 43.45km (27mls)! He thereby achieved the longest continuous crawl on record. **Why not try a scaled-down version, say 100m against the clock, with some friends.**

1.

START

2.

Rubik riddle

16 year old Vietnamese refugee Minh Thai beat all comers at the 1982 World Rubik Cube Championships in Budapest, Hungary. His winning time, after standardised dislocations, was 22.95 seconds. Given that there are 43,252,003,274,489,856,000 possible combinations, this was a quick bit of cubism! **Get out your stop-watch and see what your own best time is for solving the Rubik Riddle!**

Domino theory

Stand a load of dominoes in a line on their narrow edge and topple the first, and hey presto! the test will happily prove the Domino Theory. But this theory has been stretched by 23 year old Klaus Friedrich of West Germany. It took him a month (at ten hours a day) to set up 320,236 dominoes in January 1984 – and just 13 minutes to undo most of his work; 38,655 remained untoppled! **You'll find it hard enough to find 100 dominoes, let alone 100,000 but why not try toppling as many as you can, using curves, figures-of-eight and other patterns?**

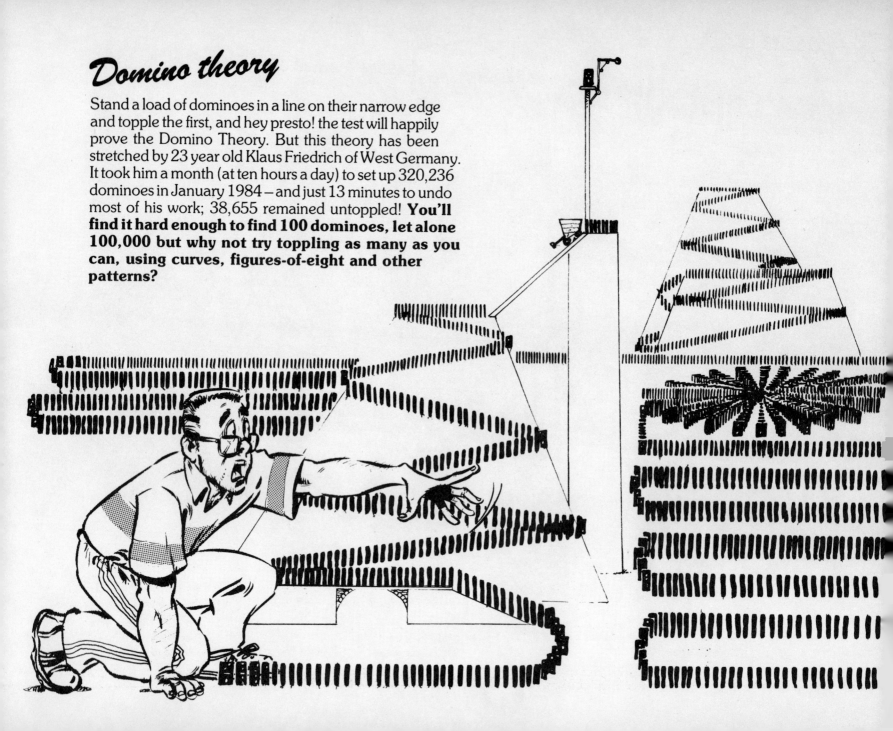

The finest cut

Who can't cut cucumbers? No one. But can you slices so finely that you get 22 cuts to the inch? Blackpool's Norman Johnson took a mere 13.4 seconds to change a 30.48cm (12in) cucumber into 224 slices in 1983. **You can try this record, *but be careful*, kitchen knives are sharp and the record is for cucumber — not finger — slicing!**

Flying eggperience

A fresh hen's egg was picked up and thrown 96.90m (317ft 10in) by Risto Antikainen; it didn't break, even when it was caught by Jyrki Korhonen! **If you try this one, make sure it's outside so no one gets egg on their face!**

DUCK'S 'N' DRAKES CONTEST — GRAND FINAL —

Stoning the water

Stone-skipping, or Ducks & Drakes, is great fun — but did you know there's a world record? It's 24 skips (10 plinkers and 14 pitty pats), held jointly by Warren Klope, John Kolar and Glenn Loy Jnr. **See how many skips you can skimmer — and just make sure the ponds big enough!**

Sunnyside up

Hopefully the golfers at a Tokyo golf club were aware of the stunt being pulled 198m (650ft) up, as David Donoghue dropped a fresh egg from a helicopter. It hit the ground unbroken – a yolk in one! **Helicopters are pricey to hire, but you might attempt a challenge from the 1st floor, as long as no one is down below!**

Shell shocked

Forget potato peeling as a kitchen work-out, and try egg shelling your way to a record – like Harold Witcomb and Gerald Harding. They shelled 1,050 dozen eggs in a 7.25 hour session in 1971. Both men were blind. **If you're egged on by this, try a speed record for half a dozen eggs – and remember to hard-boil them first!**

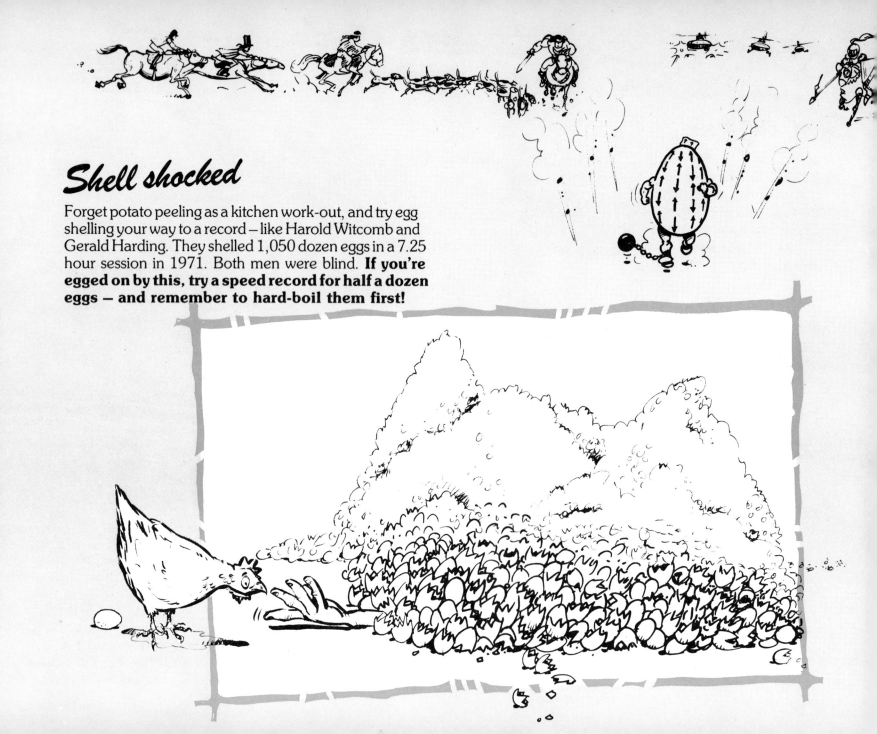

Spot the egg

Spare a thought for the egg hunters at the 25th annual Garrison Egg Hunt, Georgia, USA, who had to find 72,000 boiled eggs and 40,000 candy eggs that had been hidden! **Without cleaning out the supermarket, try your own hunt for a dozen painted, hard-boiled eggs — have a time limit, and don't hide any under cushions!**

Egghausted

In the egg and spoon Olympics, the marathon record is held by Chris Riggio of San Francisco, USA. He ran the 45.86km (28mls) in 4 hours and 34 minutes, not a bad time *without* the egg and spoon! **Try this one over a shorter distance with some friends, and see who's the best.**

What a grape catch

The ground-level grape catching record lies in the throat of American Paul Tavilla—he caught the flying fruit after it was thrown from 82.4m (270ft) away! **Why not buy a bunch of grapes and see who can catch one thrown from the furthest distance. For safety, do the catching with your hands—not your mouth!**

3. UP...UP **FOUR!**

4. FIRE... **SEVEN!**

Fore plus three...

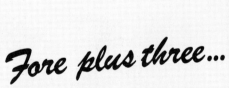

It's not as easy as it sounds, but it's worth having a go at balancing 8 golf balls vertically *without* adhesive. Lang Martin managed 7 in 1980 and went into the record books. **Go round your local golf course, collect some lost balls and get balancing.**

Tall storey

American John Sain patiently stacked a 68 storey skyscraper using over 3,000 freestanding standard playing cards! The actual height came to 3.73m (12ft 3in), and luckily no on sneezed as it was constructed. **You'd need over 70 packs of cards to equal this feat — but why not gather together what you've got and have a go?**

Wang that wellie

Wellie wanging, otherwise known as gum boot throwing, has a record holder! Tony Rodgers of Wilts., UK, threw a Dunlop size 8 Challenger boot 52.73m (173ft) in 1978. **To have a go, first get your boot — and then wang for all you are worth. Someone's going to break that record soon, and it might just be you!**

Hoop, hoop, hooray

The familiar picture of a Victorian child rolling a hoop along with stick is somewhat shattered by the modern-day marathon record set by Zolilio Diaz. He rolled a hoop 965km (600mls) from Mieres, in north west Spain, to Madrid — and back again — in 18 days! **Having a crack at such a record would tak up too much time, but why not see just how far *you* can roll a hoop — before you or it fall over!**

Hoopla

William 'Chico' Johnson hula-hooped his hips to a world record on BBC TV's *Record Breakers* in 1983, when he gyrated 81 hoops between his shoulders and hips. **The rules say that there have to be at least three complete gyrations before a record can be broken, so start swaying those hips . . . but you'll be round the bend before you come close to Kym Coberly's 72 hour single-hoop marathon!**

Get knotted ...

Get six shortish ropes, place them in a row, and on the word 'go' tie: 1 square knot, 1 sheet bend, 1 sheep shank, 1 clove hitch, 1 round turn (with two ½ hitches) and finally 1 bowline. Well, if you tie them all in under 8 seconds, you'll have secured yourself a world record – beating Clinton Bailey's 8.1 seconds, set in 1977!

1. FIND A PARTNER...

Kiss, kiss

In 1985 Eddie Leven and Delphine Crha, from Chicago, USA, joined lips for over 17 days and 9 hours – then they kissed each other, because they's broken the kissing marathon record! **Before *you* gaze adoringly into your partner's eyes, do plenty of practice puckers – and then go for a five minute kiss, and no giggling!**

2. EXERCISE YOUR MOUTH...

High as a kite

How high can you fly a kite? 10 metres? 100? 1,000? Maybe 9,740 metres (31,955ft)? Planes cruise at that height, but in 1919, in Lindenberg, now East Germany, so did a line of eight kites! **To mark exactly how far you do get your kite, attach numbered tags every metre — then read off the numbers as your kite soars up and away!**

3. PUCKER UP...

4. GET STUCK IN...

Pick up a pinta

Ahrita Furman, from New York picked up a pinta – but instead of drinking it he put it on his head and walked 38.6km (24mls) into the records. **Don't try this on with a full bottle to start with start with an empty plastic one!**

Leap de leap

A team of 14 Washington University students leaped 108,463 times over each other's backs, to cover 968.8km (602mls) – that's almost the length of Britain leap-frogged – all in 114 hours and 46 minutes! **For a more modest effort, try leap-frogging with a few friends, covering as much ground as you can before exhaustion takes over – and don't position yourself in front of a wall!**

All puffed up

One way of testing your lung-power is to see how quickly you can blow up a balloon. Now, how about blowing up a standard 1,00gm weather balloon to a 2.43m (8ft) diameter? The current holder is Nick Mason, in 1 hour, 10 minutes and 2 seconds. **Well blow me down!**

Tears for souvenirs

Alfonso Salvo broke the '50 minimum' onion-peeling record with a time of 5 minutes 23 seconds for a stack of 52 onions weighing 22.67kg (50lb)! **For your own attempt, try a couple of kilos, be careful with that knife – and no goggles!**

1. ALL ABOARD...

2. MOVE OVER ABIT PLEASE.

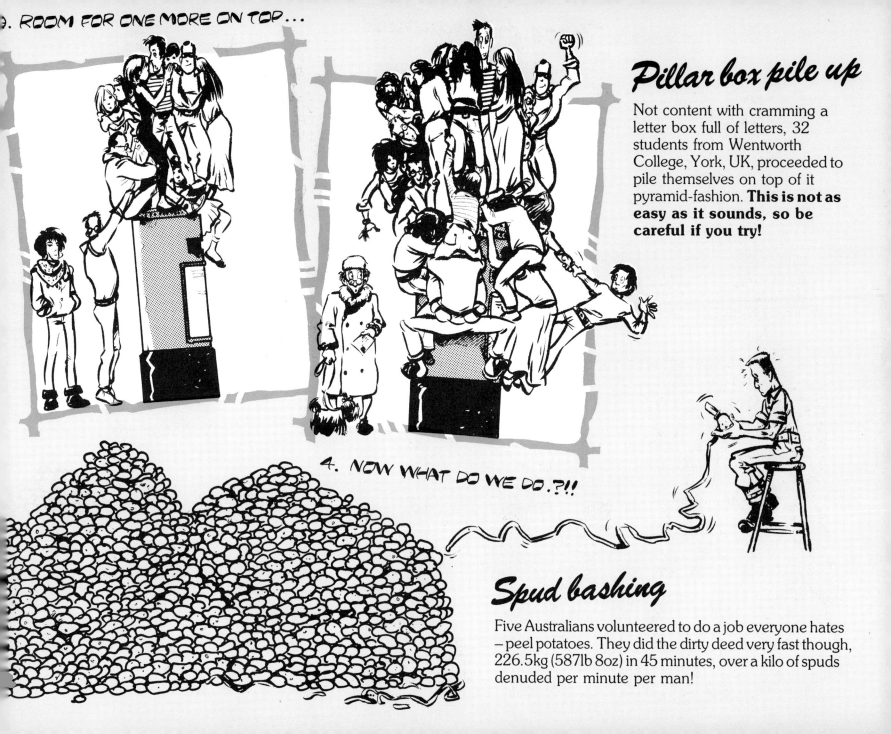

ROOM FOR ONE MORE ON TOP...

4. NOW WHAT DO WE DO.?!!

Pillar box pile up

Not content with cramming a letter box full of letters, 32 students from Wentworth College, York, UK, proceeded to pile themselves on top of it pyramid-fashion. **This is not as easy as it sounds, so be careful if you try!**

Spud bashing

Five Australians volunteered to do a job everyone hates – peel potatoes. They did the dirty deed very fast though, 226.5kg (587lb 8oz) in 45 minutes, over a kilo of spuds denuded per minute per man!

Pogoin , pogoin...

Bouncing Guy Stewart stuck to his pogo stick for 130,077 jumps during a marathon pogoing session in Ohio, USA! **On a more realistic footing, could you pogo 50 jumps without falling? Why not try it to music – Bruce *Spring*steen, maybe?**

Here's to you, Mrs. Robinson

Trying to thread cotton through the eye of a needle can be very trying . . . but Mrs Brenda Robinson had no problems threading a number 13 needle 3,795 times in two hours! **Start threading now — but watch you don't go cross-eyed!**

Dizzy dishes

We've all seen jugglers on TV shows spinning a few bits of crockery on poles – occasionally making disastrous mistakes – but Shukuni Sasaki, of Japan, managed a record-spinning 72 plates in 1981! **Your parents probably haven't got 72 plates they would wish to see smashed on the floor, so why not try with some tin plates first before graduating to the best china!**

Watchout lori's about

Whether she was aiming at some one who'd annoyed her we don't know, but Lori La Deane Adams hurled her 907g (2lb) rolling pin 53.4m (175ft 5in) at the Iowa State Fair – straight into the record books! **If you borrow your mum's to have a go, please watch out for windows!**

Roll under beethoven

So you think you can roller skate? But how about roller limboing like Denise Culp from Rock Hill, USA – she slid under a 13.33cm (5.25in) bar with only her 8 wheels touching the ground!

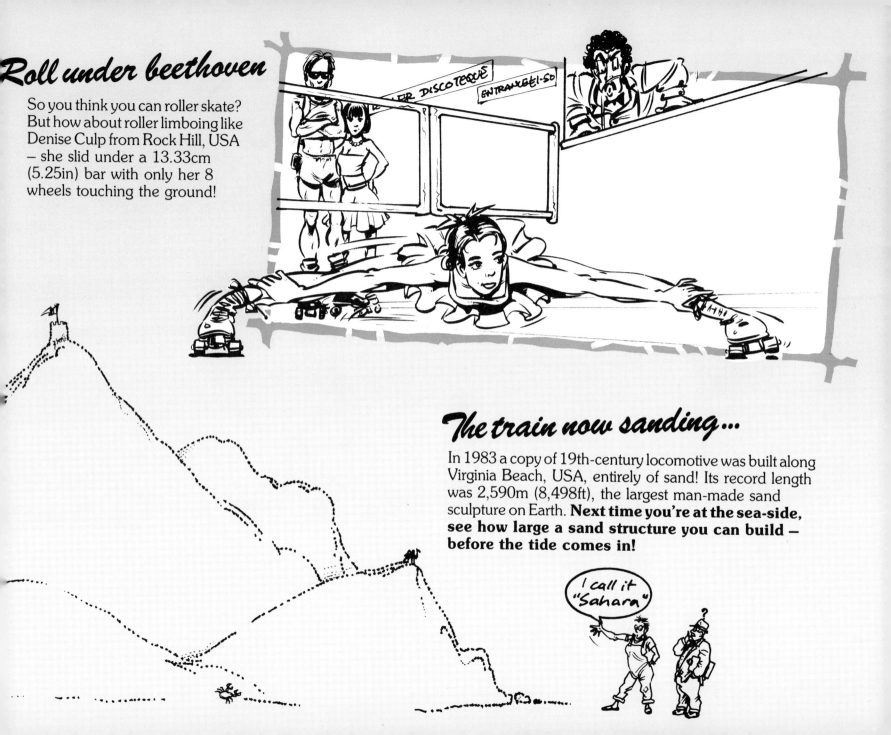

The train now sanding...

In 1983 a copy of 19th-century locomotive was built along Virginia Beach, USA, entirely of sand! Its record length was 2,590m (8,498ft), the largest man-made sand sculpture on Earth. **Next time you're at the sea-side, see how large a sand structure you can build – before the tide comes in!**

1. GURGLE... SLURP... SLOBBER...

2. SLURP... FLOOOOOP... DING!

FLOOP!

A hop, spit and a jump

At the Spittin', Belchin' and Cussin' Triathlon in Colorado, USA, you can gob into the record books with almost anything – melon seeds are popular, and the record is 19.91m (65ft 4in), set John Wilkinson in 1980. Why n try with grape pips? – but practi somewhere *private!*

Top spin

Remember spinning tops? Usually a cone or pear-shaped metal toy that you rotate on its sharp point – *that* sort of spinning top! Well, Peter Hodgson span one a staggering 58 minutes and 20 seconds in 1985 . . . not a lot of people can do that!

Shattering shouts

"Hear ye . . . hear ye!! The Town Crier National Contest has been won most often by Ben Johnson – eleven times between 1939 and 1973!" **Obviously something to shout about, but trying out your own shout requires tact – choose a large open space and, with some friends, see who can be heard from the furthest distance.**

Stamp-ede!

Comedian Frankie Howerd's tongue is a record-breaker, you may be surprised to learn! The star of stage and screen is in the *Guinness Book of Records* for using it to lick and stick 72 stamps to envelopes in under a minute, at the Post Office's inaugural contest in 1984. **Now's your chance to have the last lick — but make sure you put the stamps on blank envelopes so they won't be wasted!**

One step at a time

Climbing stairs to break records — like Dennis Martz's 11 minutes 23.8 seconds for the 100 storey Detroit Plaza Hotel — is only for the strong of heart; but for stair climbing endurance, Bill Stevenson has climbed up the Houses of Parliament tower 4,000 times in 15 years — equivalent to stepping up Everest nearly 30 times! **Try and run up and down your stairs in 30 seconds — but try and do it ten times!**

Skipping school

There are a many skipping records – non-stop marathon (12 hours and 8 minutes by Frank Oliveri, USA, 1981), most turns in a minute (330 by Brian Christensen, USA, 1979), most turns in 10 seconds (128 by Albert Rayner, UK, 1982) – but how about the team event on a single rope? This record is held by a school team of 90, in Japan, which skipped 97 times in 1983 before falling down! **How many friends could you get together for a record attempt? It'll all depend on how long your skipping rope is!**

Are you sitting comfortably?..

A record 10,323 people – all employees of the Nissan Motor Company, Japan – sat down on each other's knees, thus establishing the largest unsupported circle yet recorded! **You can try out this physical paradox of sitting without a chair by getting 10 or more friends together for a go.**

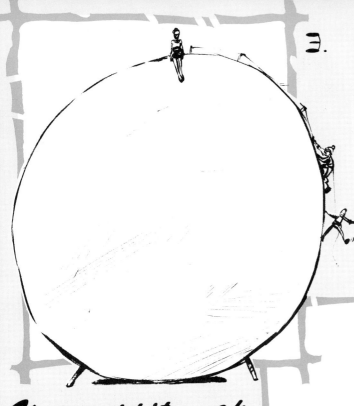

Stringalongaball

American Francis Johnson must have had quite a bit of spare time on his hands – he made an amazing 3.88m (12ft 9in) diameter, 12.9m (40ft) circumference, 10 ton ball of string between 1950–78! **Unless you plan to spend the next 28 years at it, you should compete to see who can collect the biggest ball of string in one week.**

Yap, yappity, yap

The traditional after dinner speech was turned into a record-breaking marathon at a Liverpool hotel in 1985, when Paul Osgood spoke for a tortuous 16 hours and 16 minutes. He was still waffling on at breakfast-time! Whether the guests were nodding their heads in agreement, or just nodding off, isn't clear. **A simpler non-stop talking test might be to try speaking on any subject without deviation, hestitation or repetition for a minimum of 60 seconds.**

Iced lighting

Tony Dowdeswell consumed 1.530kg (3lb 6oz) of unmelted ice cream in 50.04 seconds, at the Cardinal Wolsey Hotel, Surrey, UK, in 1984. The flavour wasn't specified, and the bill must have melted his pocket!

Beanz meanz...phew!

The gluttony record for eating baked beans – individually, using a cocktail stick (how refined) – in 30 minutes is 2,780! The windy winner was Karen Stevenson of Merseyside, UK, in 1981.

Prunes...pardon!

They say prunes are marvellous at getting things going, so perhaps jelly-man Peter Dowdeswell needed some help when he hogged down 144 prunes in 34 seconds in Suffolk, UK, in 1984! **No one seems to know how you _stop_ prunes working though!**

Wibbly...wobbly

The Dowdeswell family are apparently no novices when it comes to devouring food wholesale; Peter Dowdeswell gulped down 56.8c.lt (20fl oz) of jelly in 13.11 seconds at Stoke Mandeville, Bucks, UK, in 1984. It's a shame the two brothers didn't do a joint attempt – ice cream and jelly go together so well!

Sandwich scavenger

Before he polished off all the prunes and jelly, Peter Dowdeswell had already eaten his way into the records by scoffing down a mere 40 jam sandwiches (each 15.2×9.5×1.3 cm, 6×3.75×0.5in) in 17 minutes 53.9 seconds. Strangely enough, he did the deed in a donut shop in California, USA!

Crisp cruncher

A couple of packets of crisps will usually satisfy a snack-hungry stomach, but obviously not Paul Tully's – in May 1969 he munched through 30 packets of crisps in 24 minutes and 33.6 seconds at Melbourne University, Australia. **And he did it without a single drink!**

Banana battler

You wouldn't expect a doctor to make gluttony record attempts, but Dr Ronald Alkana, of the University of California, USA, gobbled up 17 bananas – each a minimum 128g (4½oz) edible weight – in two minutes flat in 1973. **Over two pounds a minute!**

Spaghetti slurper

Jelly, prunes and sandwich glutton Peter Dowdeswell also slurped up 91.44m (100yds) of spaghetti in 21.7 seconds at the Globe Hotel, Northants, UK, in 1983. With or without bolognaise sauce is not recorded.

1. SELECT FOUR FINGERS...

2. BLOW HARD...

3. LISTEN... WAIT...

Whistle while you work...

David 'Harpo' Hall whistled his way to a non-vinyl record by completing a marathon 25 hour whistle on a San Francisco TV show on 1st April 1983. Anyone tuning in midway would probably have thought there was a fault in their set! **You might try a shorter attempt – perhaps a five minute whistle to start with – but remember to keep your lips well lubricated!**

Sweet selling success

The world's best-selling sweets are the hole-in-the-middle *Lifesavers* – over 29½ thousand million have been sucked between 1913 and 1980. Placed end-to-end, or hole-to-hole, that would make a tunnel that stretched to the moon and back three times! **Why not see how long you and your friends can make your favourite centreless mint last before it breaks – if you crack 7 hours and 10 minutes, then you've broken American Thomas Syta's 1983 record!**

Fastest dart in the world

Have you got a dartboard? Then stand at arm's length and throw one dart 'around the clock', going only for doubles – ie. the outer circle. If you can throw a complete circle in under 9.2 seconds, you will have beaten the record set by Dennis Gower at the Miller's Arms public house, Hastings, UK, in 1975!

Football control crazy

It's a good test of your co-ordination skills to see how many times you can juggle a football using only feet, legs and head – without letting the ball touch the ground. Robert Walters took ball control out of this world with his stunning non-stop 13 hours and 2 minutes in 1984.

Potty training

The origins of the game of tiddlywinks are uncertain, but one thing is sure – the record for potting 24 'winks' from 45cm (18in) away is 21.8 seconds, set by a 20 year old, Stephen Williams, in 1966. The record still hasn't been broken! **So why don't all you budding tiddlywinkers get going and see how many 'winks' you can pot in under 30 seconds!**

2. WINK AT THE TIDDLY...

1. TIDDLE YOUR WINK...

Too marble-ous for words

The game of marbles was invented by the Romans in the 1st century AD, but it took more than 1,000 years before it became an established sport. The British Championship has been won 20 consecutive times by the **Toucan Terribles** – 1956 to 1975!

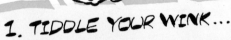

3. DO BATTLE...' THE WIDDLY OF THE TINKS'.

Fast forward...in reverse!

Bet you didn't know that running backwards has its champions! The fastest backwards mile is 6 minutes 7.1 seconds, held by Donald Davies of the USA, and the about turn 100 yards is held by American Freddie Adoboe in a time of 12.8 seconds. The endurance record goes to Anthony 'Scott' Weiland for a 4 hours, 7 minute marathon! **As this is a bit like running with your eyes shut,** *be careful,* **do it somewhere safe — not the open road!**

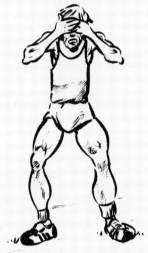

Handstanding achievement

If sprinting backwards sounds difficult, what about inverted sprinting? US Airman Thomas Hunt hand-sprinted 50m (54.7yds) in 18.4 seconds in 1979 – but this pales into insignificance beside John Hurlinger's record walk from Vienna to Paris, averaging 2.54kph (1.58mph) for just under two months. **All on his hands, of course!**

How charming can you get?

Earthworms can be attracted to the surface by using vibrations — and in a sporting version of this, called 'worm charming', a record 511 worms were charmed right out of their 9 sq.m (10.76 sq.yd) plot of land in 30 minutes. The record breaker's name? Tom Shufflebotham. Maybe that was his secret weapon! **Whatever your surname, why not get out into the garden and have a go with a square metre of worm-filled turf!**